Jasmine's Letters from God

MICHAEL CARLUCCIO

TABLE OF CONTENTS

(Letters from God are numbered)

Introduction

Jasmine is my son Paul's oldest daughter. She has two younger brothers and one younger sister. She was a bright, very talkative and loving 10 year old girl, who was going through a somewhat difficult transition from childhood to adolescence, when I decided to ease her way by writing letters and telling her they came, through me to her, from God. She has a strong belief in the power of God. The letters span her tenth year with the last one written for her eleventh birthday.

My intention in writing these letters was to teach myself and others, through Jasmine's emerging adulthood and childlike trust, to discover the power of Our One Creator God Who flows easily through us as we are willing to have the obstacles of mistrust and fear washed clean by Holy Spirit.

Although these letters are written to a ten year old, it is my intention that these letters will also be read by adults, not merely as letters meant for children, but as letters meant for the innocently loving child within us all,

that child that loves to play and is serious about its play,

that child that is trustingly innocent in its approach to life,

that child that is naturally joyful and laughs frequently and often for no apparent reason.

Children are in the ongoing process of becoming.

Children are naturally open to love.

Children know that they don't know what anything is for.

They naturally ask to get answers and directions.

Children are born with few rules.

They consciously open themselves to not know who or what they are.

They ask to learn what everything is for.

They ask to learn where they come from.

They are willing to discover, through an emptiness they desire to fill, what is presently before them.

The invitation offered by these letters is to innocently notice the truth of ourselves. With our willingness to become in spirit like an innocent child we can learn from our higher self where truth is and allow this truth to flow as desire and passion.

This point of view corresponds to Jesus' comment in the Christian gospels that we must become like little children to inherit the kingdom of Heaven.

Augustine, fourth century founder of Augustinian monks, had a short rule for his followers which could be stated as the rule guiding these letters and a rule guiding unencumbered childlikeness "Love, and do what you will. If you keep silence, do it out of love. If you cry out, do it out of love. If you refrain from punishing, do it out of love. Let the root of love be within. From such a root nothing but good can come."

1. Little Nancy

Dear Jasmine,

Here is a little story I made up to help you understand how you and I are related:

One very clear, starry night a small child, called Nancy , asked her mother how her small eyes could ever see God.

Her mother replied, "Come with me, Nancy, outside and let us look up at the sky." This they eagerly did.

"What do you see?" her mother asked.

Nancy replied, "I see a lot of stars that are so bright they all seem to be one star. They light up the whole sky."

"Is this Heaven?" Nancy asked.

"Yes it is." Her Mother replied.

"But where do your eyes put this heaven?," her mother continued.

Nancy thought for an instant and blurted out, "Inside me!"

"Yes," responded her mother, "Your small eyes brought all of heaven into you."

She continued, "Do your eyes seem small now?"

"No," replied Nancy, "my eyes must be as big as Heaven."

They hugged and happily went back into their home, bringing all of Heaven with them.

"Be talking again with you tomorrow.

Till then, see you in Heaven."

God

Drawing by Sandra

Little Nancy Plays with God

She reaches for the stars to pull them in.
They say no, no, "That's not a win."
Instead they pull her out.
They want to play her all about.

In and out, out and in,
Between and through
Over and under
So much to do.

She laughs with glee,
So much to see.
The stars are sparkling, gleaming lights.
But what is this?
In what's not seen there's more delight.

There's something in between
that tickles her and makes her scream.
I got you now she hollers.
You've been hiding between the stars and flowers.

I know you now
Don't take a bow
Because I too can love what's
In between my friendly stars, my friendly flowers.
I see you sowing love between

And making tickling joys,
I too love these many ways and things we play
in our heavenly box of toys .

Michael

2. Miracles

Dear Jasmine,

Did you notice any miracles yesterday?

I bet you didn't call them miracles but,

Did someone smile at you?

Did someone play with you?

Did you look in the mirror and see a beautiful face?

Did you look around the room and see all the things that bring you joy?

These are all miracles because you let your spirit join with what appears outside of you.

That's what my miracles do. They help you become part of and enjoy all my creations.

Do you know you can make miracles for others too?

You can smile at them.

You can play peacefully with them.

You can teach them something they don't know.

You can let them know how much you appreciate them.

You can let them know how much you love them.

Whatever you give others you will receive for yourself

Till tomorrow, think of what I wrote to you today,

I love you,

God

3. Angels

Dear Jasmine,

In the last letter I talked to you about how there are miracles around you all the time. You just have to look with your heart to experience them.

Today I would like to talk to you about angels. They are always around as well. They are bundles of light that can move anywhere without effort.

You might find them in your dreams or when you are being very still. Or they may come to you when you are taking a test in school or playing your saxophone. They help you get the right answers. They help you play beautiful songs.

Sometimes angels will take human or animal or plant or even rock forms. They can take any form that will bring light and beauty and truth to your world.

And here is a surprise for you. You are an angel who has forgotten that you decided to come to this earth to bring, beauty, light and music. I see the beautiful pictures you draw of yourself. I hear the beautiful music you play. I know you extend love to everyone you meet.

Love,

God

Here is a little story one of my other angels wrote for you telling how you as an angel became Jasmine the 10 year old girl you are today:

How You Came to Be

Dear Jasmine,

Long, long ago, before there was even sand in the hourglass, there was a teeny, tiny dot, called Jasmine – so small it was virtually invisible – that was presented to you, one of God's angels, as a gift.

At first, puzzled and perplexed, you thought it was a joke. Yet, trusting and inquisitive, your intuition led you to accept it and, before long, to carefully examine it.

And lo, after becoming extraordinarily teeny and tiny yourself, you found there was an entrance of sorts into this little treasure, in the form of a long and winding path. So inside you went, through the densest grove of ancient, moss-covered, bending oaks you will ever see, and before long, you found a shiny, gold, old-fashioned key that had been left upon a large, rounded stone, as if especially for you.

With key in hand you proceeded down the path until you arrived at a massive gate. Just above it there was a handwritten plaque for all who might pass beneath it:

"Welcome to the Jungles of Time and Space, where nothing is as it seems, yet all things are possible. Should you ever feel lost or weary, forget not from where you have come, and follow the signs..."

Peering between the wrought iron bars, you could see the entire Milky Way Galaxy and a hundred billion galaxies beyond it. Your thoughts raced, your imagination ran wild, and as you raised your key to the sturdy, reinforced lock, slowly slipping it in, and gently turning... there was a sudden flash of light and burst of sound. Whereupon, seemingly light-years later but, in fact, no longer than an instant, you found yourself in the most beautiful human form, living on the most beautiful little planet, having a wonderful life, a wrinkle of curiosity on your brow, reading this very note, right here and now, as Jasmine.

Remember
Thoughts become things... choose the good ones!

Angel Elanthra

4. Second Letter on Angels

Dear Jasmine,

I know you believe in angels. I'm glad you do because they are real. More real than the things you see with your body's eyes. Your body's eyes only give you a reflection of reality.

Angels are seen with the heart's eyes. Love is what brings them close to you. They are always around you but only when you are willing to express your love do they speak to you. You see, they respect your freedom to experience only what you wish at any time.

Don't be afraid to speak with them. Often they will come while you are sleeping because a lot of fearful distractions are not present. I suggest that you think of them just before you are about to fall asleep and ask them any questions you may want answered. They will come to bring you the answers. You have My word on this.

We'll see you in your dreams.

Love,

God and His angel friends

Digital Angel

Jasmine,
Angels can take any form that
will bring light and beauty
and truth to your world.

Even a cactus can contain an angel's energy. Always ask to
see the more that something is being.

Never take for granted what it is you think you see.

Our eyes deceive us with appearances that never contain
the whole truth

of the moment we're experiencing.

If you find yourself in the hot desert and walk by a saguaro
cactus, always

remember God's love is flowing through you from
everywhere, even a cactus.

Digitally created and written by

Angel Sandy

Angel Light

Angel's Light follows you wherever you
may go. Look for it in this picture;

Photo taken by Angel Laura

5. Loving Is Allowing

Hello Jasmine,

I want to thank you for your willingness to talk with me.

It may seem as though I am doing all the talking but I listen to your heart all the time.

I hear all the loving thoughts that reside there and for these I am so grateful to you.

I created you with a free will.

That means that you don't have to listen or speak to me if you choose not to.

I always respect your free will, since I am the One who gave it to you.

I would never force you to think, do or feel any special way.

If you seem to be closed to Me, I just wait until I sense an opening in your heart for Me.

You see, I am always there in your heart waiting for such an opening

and I promise you I will always be there for all eternity.

That is how you and I are joined as One.

I love you so much,

God

6. Having Fun with My Beautiful World

Dear Jasmine,

Look around you. There is beauty all about.

Enjoy the beauty I send you. Have fun with it.

Here are some photos Pop Pop took on one of his walks with his dog, Teacup.

Can you see a space ship there?

Can you see an angel there?

What else can you see?

Ask your friends what they see.

Ask your Mom and Dad what they see.

Have fun!

Try finding things that you think are beautiful, like the clouds in the sky.

Have fun! Make up stories about them.

Your fun loving pal,

God

7. My Love Helper

Hello Jasmine,

It is so good to be able to talk with you today.

Did you know that whatever you think about effects everyone in your world?

When you have happy thoughts others feel happy.

When you have beautiful thoughts others feel beautiful.

When you have a loving thought others experience the warmth of your love.

It's like you could be with yourself and also be with them at the same time.

You are being my helper when you have such thoughts and feelings.

Will you help me today by having happy, beautiful and loving thoughts?

See how often you can do this today.

Good feelings will follow.

Remember, I am with you even if you are having sad, ugly or unloving thoughts.

These just push me within you until you are willing to give up the sad,

ugly and unloving thoughts. It only takes your willingness. You need do nothing more.

Then I pop up with happiness, beauty and love for you and everyone.

Always remember I love you, just as you are, and I wish for you to do likewise for others,

God

8. Trust Yourself - Trust Me

Dear Jasmine,

I'm going to tell you something that may seem strange, but I want you to test it in your own life, not just take my word for it.

Avoiding something, Jasmine, draws it ever near.

Like when you avoid cleaning your room. Doesn't it stay on your mind, and doesn't it seem to always get messier? And when somebody seems to be attacking you, doesn't defending yourself and

attacking them cause them to seem to attack more? Defending yourself can become a full time job. And, also, worrying about things that might never happen increases the chances of them happening.

You see, what you keep foremost in your mind is more likely to show up then what you don't think about. That's why I always tell you to think of beautiful and happy things. If you do, they are more likely to show up for you.

Remember, I want only your happiness and if you trust me that is what you will have.

So there is no need for avoiding anything, defending against anything or worrying about anything.

Trust! Trust! Trust! is all I ask you to do.

Your loving friend,

God

9. Being in More than One Place at the Same Time

Dear Jasmine,

Today I am going to speak to you about being in more than one place at the same time. If this seems strange to you, it is because you think of yourself as your body and bodies can only be in one place at one time. But you are not your body.

Let me explain a bit:

Do you ever experience someone you love as being very close to you even though they may be

miles away? Pop Pop told me that many times he experiences being with you in New Jersey when he

is in North Carolina at his computer typing these letters for Me to send to you. Do you ever

experience him when you read My letters? This is an example of being in two places at the same

time. You are at home in your room and with Pop Pop in North Carolina in his home at the same time.

Do you like experiencing this kind of thing? I know you sometimes do.

As God, I am in all places, all the time, at the same time. For now, you can sometimes experience being in many places at the same time. Some day you will be like Me and be able to do it all the time.

Would you like to do this more often?

I'm sure you would like to because you know it increases your joy and happiness.

Here's one way to increase this ability:

Say every day, as many times as you can remember, these words:

> "I am loved.
>
> I am loving.
>
> I am loveable now and forever."

Keep saying these words until they become very true for you.

That's all you need do. I will do the rest.

Do you think you can do this?

I know you can, and I know you will.

I love my lovable Jasmine, and I know she loves Me and others,

God

10. Blessings to Share

Dear Jasmine,

I would like to speak to you today of "Blessings."

I would like you to send out your "Blessings" to the whole world.

This is the reason I created you, for I know that as you bless others you are blessing yourself.

Now let me tell you what some meanings of "Blessings" are:

To bless is:

1. To make someone or something holy in your mind and heart.

2. To pray for someone to have joy and well being.

3. To give of yourself fully to another in love.

4. To make someone happy.

5. To make the "sign of the cross" over someone, when this "sign of the cross" means that you wish someone to join in bliss with Me and your brothers and sisters right now.

When you say "In the name of the Father" you are calling forth God's Mind and your own. When you say "In the name of the Son", you are joining God's Mind with God's Heart and with yours. And when you say " In the name of the Holy Spirit" you are bringing all of God's creation into union with God's and your mind and heart.

6. To give someone a gift.

Remember, as you give these "Blessings", you will receive them.

All these "Blessings" come from me and are always there for you but you don't know this unless you give them away.

And remember to have fun doing this. Always have fun in whatever you do and don't make anything too serious. Know that I am with you "all the way".

Love ya',

God

11. More Blessings

Dear Jasmine,

In a previous letter I talked to you about "blessings." I explained what some people think that blessings are and told you that when you gave away blessings you were gaining more blessings for yourself. Let's see how this works.

Your Daddy was given the blessing of being able to build very beautiful additions to houses. When he does this, the owners of the houses feel very blessed to have such beauty to live in. They then ask him to build more additions and tell their friends who also ask him to build more additions.

Your mother was blessed with a very caring heart. She is calm and peaceful when caring for her children. You all benefit by being at peace and feeling loved. You then find it easy to love others and to bring peace into the world. This makes your mother feel very warm and peaceful inside.

Your brother, Paul was blessed with an ability to learn things easily and to be very good at games and sports. People enjoy playing with him not only because he is good at what he does but is always fair to them. This makes it easy for him to find others to play with.

You are talented in art and music. When you share these blessings with others they are very happy. Others let you know your art and music make them happy. They thank you for sharing your art and music. You then want to give away these blessings even more.

I'm sure you can also find the blessings that your sister, Jade and brother, Jacob have been given by Me. Everyone you know has been given some blessings. Look today and notice the blessings that others have been given and notice how when they give these away everyone else is blessed. That's the way My gifts work. They have to be given away to bless. If you hide them they do not bless and you and your world become sad. We can always change this sadness to gladness by sharing but while sadness lasts it hurts.

So today be thankful for the blessings I gave you and notice the blessings I give others. Enjoy all these blessings as if they all belong to you. They do belong to you. You know this is true when you and others share these blessings with one another.

Accept My blessings of Love,

God

Beauty

Dear Jasmine,

I believe we are blessed when we have the time to stop
doing and just

enjoy the peace of a beautiful sunset.

Laura

Soul Touches Soul

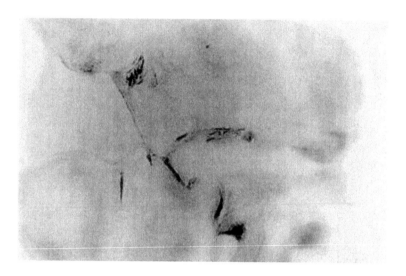

Dear Jasmine,

One of my many blessings is, my grand-daughter, Holly's, birth in February 2006.

I drew/painted, this from a photograph of my oldest son having a "blissful blessing-filled moment" with his newborn daughter.

I send out another blessing from my heart to another grand-daughter who has just been born. This will be my second grand-daughter. Her name is MacKenzie, and this is a blessing straight from God into my family's heart.

Sandy

12. Today Is a Day for Dreaming

Dear Jasmine,

Today is a day for day dreaming. I mean dreaming with your eyes open. I mean imaginatively creating what you would like your life to be. Drink in your dreams with joy. Relish them. Savor them. Taste delightfully the texture of your dreams.

This is the stuff of which your future is made. You may dream of a pretty red dress and get a blue one or no dress at all, but so what. The dream was fun was it not. Everything you see, hear, smell, taste, experience in your world has been dreamt up by you. You may not remember dreaming it up but I assure you, you did.

Now if something shows up that you don't like, don't sweat it. You can change the dream to one you like by just seeing things differently. And you can choose a different dream if you like. So, be a dreamer of humongous dreams, dreams that make your head spin, dreams that delight you to no end. And remember this, I will always be here for you when you get tired of dreaming and just want to create new worlds with Me. This is even greater fun than dreaming.

See you in your dreams,

God

13. You Are Beautiful. You Are Loving. You Are Lovable.

Dear Jasmine,

Do you know that everyone who comes into your life was sent by Me? I sent them to help you learn to love yourself completely. Treat each one as a guest in the home of your heart.

You can learn a lot about this from your mother and father. Notice how they treat guests in their home. Notice how they treat Pop Pop. They give him their own room, the best room in the house. They take him with you and your brothers and sister to places they think he will enjoy. They cook and prepare delicious meals for him. They encourage him to play with you and your brothers and sister. They provide anything he needs to be comfortable in their home. He so appreciates this that he returns all the love he has to them and to you.

This is how I want you to treat everyone who comes into your life, even those who seem tough and obnoxious. They are soft and tender underneath but are very frightened that they might reveal the love that is within them. You love and respect them in any way you can. They will get it even if they don't show that they do. I guarantee this.

You will benefit regardless of how they react. You will be learning to know how loving, lovable and beautiful a person you are.

You are my angel and I love you,

God

14. I Love You Just the Way You Are

Dear Jasmine,

Do you know what a judge does? He looks at the evidence. He decides what is right and what is wrong. He decides if someone is guilty or if someone is innocent.

When we say someone is prejudiced we mean that he judges without evidence. He jumps to conclusions before he ever sees the evidence for guilt or innocence, for right or wrong.

We can also say that when someone plans for the future, he is making decisions or judgments that if something happens the way he would like it to happen he will be happy. He tries to make it happen the way he wants it to happen and may become quite upset if things don't turn out the way he planned.

You do all these kinds of judging, right. Almost all people living or have ever lived act and think this way at times.

Here's what most people don't know. This judging is what makes you sick, makes your mind go crazy and makes your muscles get tight and your stomach turn about. Things in your body get clogged up. Sometimes it even makes it difficult for you to have regular bowel movements. Do you ever experience any of these problem? I know you have.

The messages and letters that I send you are meant to help you stop all these judgments, and I mean all of them! There is only one judgment I ever make and only one I want you to ever make about yourself and others. You are a perfect creation, just the way you are. I also judge everything in your world as perfect, just the way it is. When you think or feel otherwise give these thoughts and feelings to Me. I will put them in my cleansing machine and wash them clean for you. They will come back to you as loving thoughts about yourself and everything in your world.

By giving up judgment, making decisions on your own without Me, giving up planning and trying to manipulate the future, the result will be miracles all around for everyone. I promise you.

Love ya' just the way you are,

God

Response to letter about loving yourself just the way you are

It is a real pity that everyone can't "handle" this message. I taught it to my daughter when she was in Kindergarten. She and I would sing to an audio tape of Louise Hay's, a musician had written the song "I love myself just the way I am" with lyrics that went on to say:

I love myself just the way I am

There is nothing I need to change,

I'll always be the perfect me,

There's nothing to rearrange,

I'm beautiful and capable

Of being the best me I can

And I love myself

Just the way I am!

I taught her to sing it loud and proud. It took all of one school day for her to get into my car and demand from me why I didn't explain to her that she should NEVER sing that in front of anyone else! She was as mad as I've ever seen a 5 year old.

I still laugh about it. Her, not so much. Thanks for the memory of that wonderful song!

Love

Sonja

15. Follow up Letter to "I Love You Just the Way You Are."

Dear Jasmine,

I want to say some more about loving yourself just the way you are. Everyone I have created is different from everyone else. Even though people seem alike in many ways no two are alike in all ways. Look at people closely. No two bodies are exactly alike. This is true even in twins.

One person may be tall, another short. One loves a certain movie, and another does not. One speaks French, another English. One has brown eyes, one has blue.

Let me say something about these eyes. These many eyes, though different, all have one purpose: to connect with others. Remember, no matter what color or shape the eyes, when eyes look into another's eyes, the soul is seen, love is experienced. Eyes are meant to meet for this purpose. They are meant to look deep and see the universe of love that resides outside the loneliness sometimes felt within.

Do you remember when you and Pop Pop looked into one another's eyes? Do you remember the love you felt? Pop Pop told me he would never forget it. The last time he visited you, he said he got you to smile when you were angry by just reminding you of this love contact you two made with your eyes.

It's the surprise we feel in connecting to what seems to be outside of us that we call a miracle of love. If we were not all different we could never experience this surprising feeling.

Since it brings love what could be more wonderful than differences? Who would not seek them rather than sameness? Who would want to erase differences from the face of the Earth? Not I. I bless them. I love all differences alike, because I know the joy we all experience when we combine the differences. Let differences be enjoyed! Let differences be celebrated!

What a waste of time and energy it would be to try to make yourself be like someone you admire. It would kill love. It is okay to admire someone else for being the way they are, but don't forget to admire yourself just the way you are.

And when differences join together to make something the differences blend together to create something new, something wonderful, something beautiful, something surprisingly delightful. It's like when you make a soup, the soup benefits from all the ingredients. Who can say that the carrots are more important than the potatoes? Which ingredient from a wonderful soup would you choose to remove? Leave in all the flavors. They can only add to the richness of the soup.

See how many soups you can make today by joining with others in whatever way you can. Enjoy it all. And don't forget to love what you bring to the pot.

Loving all of you,

God

Perfection Personified

How can you question, how can you doubt
Very few of my children know what life's about
How can you think I'd rain down torment
You should know in your heart, it isn't God-sent.

I created each soul in a state of perfection
You've become what you are by your own mind's projection
If you think you're a failure then check your own thoughts
And know you have purchased just what you have sought.

The path you are on you have chosen to walk
Life is the blackboard, free will is the chalk.
Nothing in life is predestined by fate
Is fate a world filled with corruption and hate?

I created perfection, you created hell.
Why go on clanging the same misery bell.
You are the center of your own universe
With such creative powers so very diverse.

I created all matter, I created expanse
Every start that IS in the Great Cosmic Dance.
Look at the heavens the story is told
A great wondrous site, a gift to behold.

Look at your children and know in your heart
They came from your body, of me they're a part.
Why treat my flowers as if they are weeds.
Recognize very quickly they all are my seeds.

You moan and you cry and you call out my name,
when life is downtrodden ~ when life is mundane.
How often when life is cresting a peak,

Do you seek me out or with me want to speak.

I created your world and gave you free will.
You were a spark cast out, aware of nothing until
Consciousness awareness was breathed in your soul
Until that time you were a part of the WHOLE.

I gave you freedom to experience life,
when I gave to Adam the first human wife.
From that day forward you've had free reign,
and it is YOU that have chosen your misery and pain.

Look within to see where you are.
Look within again, I'm not very far.
Know that your faith will lead you to me,
The faith that's been buried in your polluted seas.

Look in a child's eyes to find innocence.
Start from the bottom and try to make sense,
out of the chaos and frustration with life,
harmony is waiting, get rid of your strife.

Take time out of schedules to glimpse a rainbow.
Sit out at dusk when the sun's setting low.
Count up the wonders I've placed on your earth.
Think of my best, the wonder of birth.

Looks at the animals I've placed by your side.
How can you humans let so many die?
You ignore their plight, you kill them for food.

What I had in mind you have misunderstood.

What of my churches and what they represent.
A place for sinners to attend and repent.
A place to worship an untoucheable God.
A place to flock, to nap and nod.

You don't need a church to link with the source.
You don't need to miss church and then feel remorse.
Take a few minutes from some of your tasks,
to talk with me daily, is all that I ask.

I remember each soul as a new vibrant spark
Awaiting the challenge to make their own mark.
Their descent form the source of a nature sublime
Has seemed to erase faith in me from their mind.

Dust off the cobwebs and straighten the shelf.
Move priorities around, get to know yourself.
I will await your awakening. I'll applaud your rebirth
and while you are at it take care of my earth.

Sandy

16. More on the Foolishness of Judging

Dear Jasmine,

You have at least 5 ways to learn about things in the world. We call these the five senses; seeing, hearing, touching, smelling and tasting. You also can feel things and know things without using these senses. When you lump all of these together we call it knowing about your world through perception.

There is a problem with this, however. Knowing this way only gives you partial knowledge. That's why it is better to know that you can't ever know anything truly or fully using yourself or your body. If you learn to trust Me I will tell you the truth about things in the world a little at a time. I wait until you are ready and willing to listen and then I speak to you. You, ordinarily, have to be very still and quiet to hear Me. That's why it is good to sit in a quiet place and close your eyes and just listen. At first you will hear a lot of chatter. That's ok. Just notice the chatter and don't fight it. It soon goes away and then you will hear My Voice. Get in the habit of asking Me throughout the day, "What is this and what is it for?". I will always hear you and find a way to answer you, but remember you make it easier for Me when you are still and quiet.

Here is a poem I like and thought you might like as well. This will help you remember what I told you today. I also put in some helpful prose and a new little moral at the end that wasn't in the original poem:

Blind Men and the Elephant (a.k.a., "Blindmen")

(by John Godfrey Saxe)

American poet John Godfrey Saxe (1816–1887) based this poem, "The Blind Men and the Elephant", on a fable that was told in India many years ago.

(Six blindmen touching an elephant.)

It was six men of Indostan
To learning much inclined,
Who went to see the Elephant
(Though all of them were blind),
That each by observation
Might satisfy his mind

The First approached the Elephant,
And happening to fall
Against his broad and sturdy side,
At once began to bawl:
"God bless me! but the Elephant
Is very like a wall!"
(The first blind man of six blind men feels the side of the elephant and interprets it as a wall.)

The Second, feeling of the tusk,
Cried, "Ho! what have we here
So very round and smooth and sharp?
To me 'tis mighty clear
This wonder of an Elephant
Is very like a spear!"
(The second blind man of the six blind men feels an elephant tusk and interprets the elephant to be like a spear.)

The Third approached the animal,
And happening to take
The squirming trunk within his hands,
Thus boldly up and spake:
"I see," quote he, "the Elephant
Is very like a snake!"
(The third blind man of the six blind men touches the
elephant's trunk and interprets it to be a snake.)

The Fourth reached out an eager hand,
And felt about the knee.
"What most this wondrous beast is like
Is mighty plain," quote he;
" 'Tis clear enough the Elephant
Is very like a tree!"
(The fourth blind man of the six blind men touches the
elephant's leg and mentally visualizes it to be a tree.)

The Fifth, who chanced to touch the ear,
Said: "E'en the blindest man
Can tell what this resembles most;
Deny the fact who can
This marvel of an Elephant
Is very like a fan!"
(The fifth blind man of the six blind men touches the
elephant's ear and imagines it to be a fan.)

The Sixth no sooner had begun
About the beast to grope,
Than, seizing on the swinging tail
That fell within his scope,
"I see," quote he, "the Elephant
Is very like a rope!"

(The sixth blind man of the six blind men touches the elephant's ear and interprets it to be a fan.)

And so these men of Indostan
Disputed loud and long,
Each in his own opinion
Exceeding stiff and strong,
Though each was partly in the right,
And all were in the wrong!

Moral:

When you think you know what something is, you don't. It is only in letting "what is" reveal itself to you that you discover the many facets of its being. In this way acceptance brings you so much closer to truth than using your senses or your ego self alone to try to know the truth about anything.

I love you,

God

17. The Light in Your Heart

Dear Jasmine,

Do you like watching a fireworks display?

Do you enjoy seeing a lightening display in a distance?

Do you like seeing a brightly lit house at Christmas time?

All of these are wonderful to view, but did you know that there is a wonderful display of dancing light always available to you?

It is the Light of Love that rests in your heart and is available to you at all times.

All you need do is call it to come forth to shine in your world.

And as I said to someone recently,

"God does not speak to you for nothing. He has great purpose in mind. God is not trying to light you up. He would have you recognize your own light that is shining in your heart right now."

Love,

God

18. What Goes Around Comes Around

Dear Jasmine,

Do you like bouncing a ball on the floor or against a wall and trying to catch it on the rebound. It can be fun! It can also teach you something about how things work in the world. There is a big word for it. It is called the law of reciprocity. Some people say it this way "What goes around comes around."

The way this law works can be used to bring you great joy and happiness or it can bring you pain and misery. You see what you put into the world is what you get back.

Things that work for your happiness come from love. Things that cause misery and pain come from fear and anger. The love stuff looks like gratitude, respect, kindness, a smile, a helping hand and other things like this.

Things that don't work to bring happiness are things like getting even, hurting someone, calling names, trying to get someone in trouble. You see just like the bouncing ball all these things rebound and can come back to you.

So you see it makes so much more sense to act out of love than out of fear or anger.

Don't worry though if you make a mistake and act out of fear or anger. Just notice it and ask for my help to see things from love next time.

Remember, I am always there for you when you ask for help and I love just as much even when you make mistakes.

Your friend,

God

19. Appreciation

Dear Jasmine,

I know you love music. I hear you sing and play your saxophone so beautifully and with such heart. You were willing to sing and play for Pop Pop and Connie the last time they visited you. They so appreciated this gift from you. They also told me they enjoyed the foot rubs you love to give.

Your "Amazing Grace" was beautiful. I so appreciate when anyone appreciates the freedom we all have to bestow grace and blessings upon one another. Your doing these things for others without expecting anything in return cheers all of us in Heaven. And I bet you experience this joy since our joy is returned to you a hundred fold.

Here is a song I know you would love to sing. It is written and sung by the mother and daughter country singers called "The Judds". Pop Pop will bring you a copy of this song the next time he visits:

From the Judds:

Love Can Build a Bridge

"I'd gladly walk across the desert
With no shoes upon my feet

To share with you the last bite
Of bread I had to eat
I would swim out to save you
In your sea of broken dreams
When all your hopes are sinking
Let me show you what love means

Love can build a bridge
Between your heart and mine
Love can build a bridge
Don't you think its time?
Don't you think its time?

I would whisper love so loudly
Every heart could understand
That love and only love
Can join the tribes of man
I would give my hearts desire
So that you might see
The first step is to realize
That it all begins with you and me

Love can build a bridge
Between your heart and mine
Love can build a bridge
Don't you think its time?
Don't you think its time?
When we stand together
Its our finest hour
We can do anything, anything
Keep believing in the power

Love can build a bridge
Between your heart and mine
Love can build a bridge

Don't you think its time?
Don't you think its time?

Love and only love
Love and only love"

And from the Beatles:

"Love, Love, Love.
Love is all there is."

And you know how much I love YOU,

God

20. The Big Horseshoe Magnet in the Sky

Dear Jasmine,

I want you to look up at the stars on the next clear night. You will see trillions and trillions of stars. They make for a peaceful display of brilliant light. Everyone on earth is also a star in My Heaven. Most are not quite as bright as the stars you see in the sky right now but in time many will know themselves as one of the brightest stars in the heavens.

Here's how you can increase your BRIGHTNESS. You can join with others in love.

Love produces energy. In your world much energy is contained in magnets.

Whenever you do something loving for another you become a magnet that attracts love from many points within your world.

Love, remember, is just another word for light. Magnetism is the energy of this light and this energy is contained within all things on your earth.

I know you did some experiments in school on bar magnets and horseshoe magnets. You now know something about how these magnets work. A horseshoe magnet is much more powerful than a bar magnet. It will attract anything that contains metal. Bar magnets attract only other magnets that are opposite in polarity to them. They push away magnets that have like polarities. That's why many say unlikes attract one another.

The world has been like a bar magnet for many, many years. It is changing now to be more like a horseshoe magnet. You are helping this happen. Every time you join with someone in a loving way you strengthen this horseshoe love magnet. It just will keep growing stronger and stronger as you join in love.

Let me tell you a story of how one eleven year old girl strengthened the love magnet energy in her world.

"Come with me to a fifth grade classroom..... There is Johnny, an eleven-year-old boy sitting at his desk and all of a sudden, there is a puddle between his feet and the front of his pants are wet. He thinks his heart is going to stop because he cannot possibly imagine how this has happened. It's never happened before, and he knows that when the boys find out he will never hear the end of it. When the girls find out, they'll never speak to him again as long as he lives.

Johnny believes his heart is going to stop; he puts his head down and prays this prayer, "Dear God, this is an emergency! I need help now! Five minutes from now I'm dead meat."

He looks up from his prayer and here comes the teacher down his aisle with a look in her eyes that says he's had it.

As the teacher is walking toward him, a classmate, named Susie, is carrying a goldfish bowl that is filled with water.

Susie trips in front of the teacher and dumps the bowl of water in the boy's lap.

Johnny is startled. He wonders why Susie spilled the water all over him? He always liked Susie, she was always full of fun and always nice to him. As he looked up, he saw her wink her eye. Immediately he knew why she had done what she did. He said, 'No sweat, Susie, I know you just tripped over that pencil in the aisle. I'll be all right.'

Now all of a sudden, instead of being the object of ridicule, Johnny is the object of sympathy. The teacher rushes him downstairs and gives him gym shorts to put on while his pants dry out. All the other children are on their hands and knees cleaning up around his desk. The sympathy is wonderful. But, a small bit of the major ridicule that would have been endured has been transferred to someone else - Susie. She doesn't seem to mind.

She apologies and tries to help clean up, but the others tell her to get away.

'You've done enough, you klutz!' they say.

Finally, at the end of the day, as the kids are waiting for the bus, Johnny walks over to Susie and whispers, 'You did that on purpose, didn't you?' Susie whispers back, 'I wet my pants once too.'

That day Susie and Johnny were joined together as a horseshoe love magnet for the rest of that school year. This magnet drew many of their classmates into doing other wonderful things for others. It was the best school year that class ever had.

Susie's star was made brighter by each loving act any of their classmates did as a result of her unselfish act. It continues to grow brighter every day."

Jasmine, did you like this story? I want you to join Susie and Johnny in creating the strongest magnet of love energy the world has ever known. I know you will, and I know your star will become one of the brightest stars in our heavens. It will brighten up the starlight of many.

The Big Horseshoe Magnet in the Sky, your pal,

God

21. The Endless Ocean

Dear Jasmine,

You cried to me of how much it hurt to be called a name and teased today at school. I caught a tear and placed it in the Ocean of your own awareness. Yes! You have an Ocean!

And there, it floated about like a ripple and soon made its way, swimming about happily like the rest of the Ocean. This tear and the tears of all children who tease others, or who are teased, add to your thoughts, your dreams, which is the Ocean of Awareness. None are less valued and precious than another.

Just as this tear could no longer be seen as a separate drop of water and so could not be called names or feel hurt by names, so are you, dear, sweet Jasmine, a part of my Thoughts in the Ocean which contains all of Life and you cannot be hurt nor can you be separate from Me. You are like the winding, bubbling stream that flows into the Ocean.

You may not feel this, just yet, but some day you will. Keep offering your tears to me, turning your cheek to all your brothers and sisters who do not yet know Me and soon, you will see that all streams, including theirs, lead to this Ocean and each rock or pebble that another throws into it, can be used as a stepping stone across the stream, to where I AM. And I wait, ever patient to hold you in the Light that gives Life to this endless Ocean!

Sweet dreams Jasmine,

God

22. Your Music

Dear Jasmine,

I know you enjoy singing and playing music with your saxophone.

Your music says one word to Me, LOVE!

Your music calls Me to join you in joy.

Your music embraces Me as I listen.

Your music calls me to look into your eyes and see Myself swimming in bliss.

When I do this I know you can see Me too.

Our eyes form a duet. We blend into a song that reaches up to Heaven.

All boundaries between us break down.

We know the truth.

We are One!

Love,

God

23. War and Peace

Dear Jasmine,

Let's you and I look at anger today. I know you feel angry at times. I hear you say things to your father like, "You're not my father, I hate you." I see you do things to your brothers and sister, some times sneakily and sometimes outright that show anger. I also know that you don't like yourself later for saying these things and doing these things. I often hear you whisper to yourself, "I wish I could change, but they make me so angry sometimes."

Where is this anger? It is inside you. You can even feel it boiling inside if you pay close attention. When you spit it out onto your father or brothers or sister you are declaring war. Your peace is gone and most times the peace of others is gone as well. I don't want you to deny any of these feelings but I do want you to have a plan before anger bursts forth.

Maybe take a walk, go into your room and write a letter to the one you are angry at (then tear up the letter), sit quietly and become relaxed, put your anger into an angry drawing (then tear it up). Any of these things will work. Sharing your anger with friends is usually not a good idea if you are looking for agreement, but if you have a good friend who will tell you the truth about yourself that's another way to express your anger.

I think you get the idea. Express your anger in a way that does not declare war, in a way that does not blame, in a way that releases it and frees you to be the peaceful Self that is the true you.

If you are willing to take responsibility for your anger and do as I suggest you will be bringing peace to your world. I know you want this because in your heart I have seen this wish shining brightly.

Your peaceful and loving friend,

God

24. Having Fun Together

Dear Jasmine,

Did you know that when you are having fun playing with others I am having fun too?

I put you in this world to have fun, see and create beauty, love and be loved. That's all!

I so enjoy seeing all the different ways you all have fun, create beauty and love. I appreciate the chance to play. I so enjoy the beautiful things you make and I especially get a thrill when I experience the love you give and receive.

One thing I must mention, however, about fun. Never have fun at someone else's expense. When having fun share it with everyone who is playing with you. Even if you are playing a game of winners and losers no one is ever a loser if everyone has fun.

Have fun, create beauty and love today. Remember I am there with you enjoying it all.

Love,

God

25. Do Not Be Stingy with Your Love

Dear Jasmine,

Here is a message I adapted from one I sent my adult friends.

The world has been waiting for you. It waits for you to pour out your love. It waits for you to pour out your joy. How simple a task you have. Your heart is like a pitcher of sweet cream, and all you have to do is pour it. The more you pour the more there is to pour. The pitcher never runs out. You pour cream for the world.

The cream in the pitcher of your heart stays fresh as you pour it. It cannot curdle so long as it is ever-pouring. Pour to your heart's content. Pour out your heart's contents. Just keep pouring. Let the world swim in the outpouring of sweetness from the fullness of your heart. As you pour love out into the world, the world floats in love, and so do you. This is the stuff of the universe, the love you pour. What you pour, you drink. How simple is the universe.

This is the easy natural way to live life. There is no effort in pouring. The pitcher is light. You simply tip it and let it pour.

Do not save your heart for a rainy day. Do not be stingy with your love. Be generous instead. You are full of love. Keep pouring until the world is full of love. The entire world will bless you with joy and happiness.

This is how I love you,

God

26. Crazy Talk

My Dear Jasmine,

Do you know that you always have voices speaking to you.
This is not crazy talk, it is just the way it is.
Many of the voices are what we call ego voices.
These are the ones that try to make you feel bad.
They try to make you feel little.

They try to make you feel alone and separate from Me.

If you ever hear a voice inside say things like "you're working too slow,"

"you are too easily distracted," or

"you should take life more seriously,"

know that it absolutely, positively is not Me.

I'm the one saying, "You totally rock!"

God

Ego Teacher

The ego is a tricky little fellow.
He says go do
Then smacks our hand.
He sometimes lies
Yet wipes our tears
If we should cry.
He likes to tell us of
Science so sublime
and how it isn't mine.
He insults and
If we should throw a punch
He bends or eats our lunch.
He sometimes plays with us
At recess time.
And other times
He calls us names

He's such a tricky fellow
Cause he never tells us
That he tells us lies
That often make us cry.
He really doesn't know us well,
But wants us to think him swell.
He likes to see us fail.
He says it makes us strong.
He lies
And never wants us
To know the us that's Us.

Michael

74

Here is a poem one of my creations called Karen wrote. It tells what your world will be like if you don't listen to ego. I thought you would like it.

The Space Between

Enter the space between the stars
swinging gently in that void
let yourself be swallowed
by the vastness
where knowing is useless
and questions fall like autumn leaves
asking only to be gathered in piles
and plunged into
scattering
hooting in joy your ignorance
laughing out loud your bliss.

Enter the space between your thoughts
resting softly in the stillness
let yourself be Love
by loving All That Is
where struggles cease
and desires rise on gossamer wings
so lightly that they touch the sun
and melt away, leaving only the
faintest memories of wanting
dissolved into Being
where who you are and who I Am
are One.

27. Giving a Gift of Love

Hello Jasmine,

How would you like to give someone close to you a gift they will treasure forever? A gift that will not only make them happy but will make them want to love you even more than they do now.

Here's what you do:

1.   Before going to bed each night for one week write on a notepad all the things they did for you out of their love for you. Things like making breakfast, driving you to saxophone lessons, helping with homework, brushing your hair, buying you clothing or pokemon cards. You get the idea. Write anything they did for you that day that you know came from love. You will be amazed how many things you will find to write on your notepad.
2.   Don't tell anyone you are doing this.
3.   At the end of the week write out all the things you have noted on the fanciest paper you can find.
4.   Draw some pictures to show them doing these things.
5.   Fold the list and pictures nicely and put them in a small gift box.
6.   Wrap the box in some fancy gift paper.
7.   Write a note saying something like this:

8.   Mom, I want to thank you for loving me so much that you did all these things for me this week.

9.   Give the gift box to the one you choose.

She/He will never forget this gift and the love that they have for you will increase beyond measure.

I will be there helping you all the way.

Love,

God

28. Creating Your Own World

Dear Jasmine,

Early in the morning take some time thinking about what it is you would like to happen this day.

Write these things down.

Do this early in the morning before you do anything else.

Don't think much about what you wrote during the day.

Check at night to see how things turned out.

You will be very surprised at the results.

Your pal,

God

29. Have You Seen Me Lately?

Hello Jasmine,

Have you seen me lately? Do you know I am in everything you see?

All you have to do is look for me and you will see me.

When you look, look with your heart not your eyes or your head.

Because I am always in your heart I am in everything your heart touches.

When you find me you will be finding your true Self.

Discover yourself in the wind; hear and see Us in the gentle rain as it falls to earth; see Me sing and dance on TV.

When your heart sees it can see nothing but God because God is Love and that is what your heart sees.

And remember if God is Love so are you.

I can't help but love you because that is how I love Myself.

I am with you always, Keep you eyes open and you will always see my love pouring forth,

God

30. The Matrix

Dear Jasmine,

Did you see the movie called "The Matrix"? If you did you will remember that the hero was trying to discover that he was "The One." Do you know that you can know yourself as "The One" if you are willing to see how you are connected to everyone and everything including Me.

You can think of it this way:

I, God, am in everything you can see, hear, smell, taste, touch. I have a center or core from which I radiate out my Love to everything and everyone. My love touches everyone and everything. Whatever and whoever accepts my love will also radiate this love out into the universe, becoming "The One". Universe is just another name for "the One". So you see, like Me, God, you are in everything when you let your love radiate out to everything.

People can seem to hide from Our love but they can't stop it from being all about them. It is always there for them to see when they look with the heart's eyes. If someone or something refuses to recognize Our love they think they hide in darkness until they open their heart's eyes and see the love We are pouring forth. Those who have their heart's eyes open, however, can see that others are not really hiding only keeping their eyes shut and pretending to be hiding. It's like what little babies do when they shut or cover their body's eyes and play peek-a-boo.

31. Enjoying Every Season of Your Life

Dear Jasmine,

It's spring time. Do you hear the birds singing? Do you see the flowers blooming? Do you notice the buds on the trees? This is the time of new birth of the many forms we so enjoy. Take it all in. Feel the excitement of new birth. Enjoy! Enjoy!
Enjoy!

Summer will soon come and everything will be lush and full.

When the Fall season comes, you will see the flowers fade and appear to disappear. The trees will lose their leaves and fall to the ground.

Then winter will come and cover all with snow.

Change of form is always taking place in front of you. Enjoy it all!

The same thing happens with people. We are born as babies,grow up as children, just like you are now. Soon you will be a young adult and then continue to mature into a beautiful woman. Enjoy it all!

All of these changes can be Heaven if you are willing to enjoy it all.

This is even true when our bodies disappear. Some people call this death and think it is a sad thing. But it is just change. Don't be afraid of these changes. Even what people call dying can sometimes be only like taking off a tight pair of shoes. You free your feet so you can run and play more easily. Don't be afraid of any of these changes. I am there with you ALL THE TIME. No exception to this. Just open your heart and you will find me there.

Love,

God

32. Let Go, Let God

Dear Jasmine,

I just heard a beautiful new song written and sung by Olivia Newton John. Do you know of her? Have you every seen the movie version of the musical "Grease"?

She was the leading lady who played beside John Travolta. You may have also heard some of her music.

The title of the song is "Let Go, Let God." As you probably guessed I like it because it is about Me.

Here are the words to that song:

"Let Go, Let God.

When you can't find your directions

And your heart won't guide you home

Let Go, Let God.

When your dreams are broken in the bud

And you've lost the will to trust

Let Go, Let God.

Let the skies remind you we are passengers

Let the skies remind you to surrender

Let Go, Let God.

When the faith has died inside you

And no spark to feed your flame

Let Go, Let God.

When your courage fails you

And the well of hope runs dry

Let Go, Let God."

She had been very sick and asked Me to help. She got well from a very serious illness and was willing to let Me help her write this and other songs for her new CD. I am asking Pop Pop to get a copy and play it for you when he comes up to see you again. He will give the CD to you if you like it.

Love,

God

33. Time to Have a Party

Dear Jasmine,

I know you like to party. So do I. What I'd like you to do is party all the time. Make every moment of your life a celebration of who you really are.

When you celebrate you publicly honor Me. It's like telling everyone you know I created you and you love Me for this great gift. Some people may think you are a bit strange always being happy and full of life but, what the heck, tell them I told you to be that way. Tell them you know God wants you to have fun and to be happy so you are just going to take Him at His word.

Remember this:

Celebration is honoring God.

Celebration is honoring life.

Celebration is honoring yourself.

Till next time, party on!

Your pal,

God

34. My Laws

Dear Jasmine,

Have you ever been told to obey God's Laws? Do you know God's Laws? Some people think these are the Ten Commandments. Others, like Muslins, Jews, Buddhist, Hindus, Catholics, Methodist, Baptists, etc. add their own versions of God's Laws. Often they include rituals and dogmas that man has invented. None of these are truly My Laws.

You will find My Laws written in your heart.

Look there for what makes you happy.

That is My will for you.

That is the Law I offer you.

My Will is My Law.

And My Will is that you be perfectly happy.

Follow the will of God by having fun, giving love to everyone and everything in your world.

Do this and you will always be following My Law.

And if at times you forget and are a bit sad or mad or frightened don't sweat it.

I'm still here and am always waiting for you to awaken to the truth of My Will.

When you do "It's Party Time".

Your pal for always,

God

35. Prayer

Dear Jasmine,

I would like to talk with you today about prayer. Prayer is simply talking and listening. It is not a special thing you do, but it is life itself. Even when you seem to be talking to yourself you are praying. All prayers have answers. No prayer goes unheard or unanswered. This is why it is important to notice what conversations you are having with others and with yourself. Happy, loving conversations bring happy loving answers. Angry, fearful conversations bring angry and fearful answers. None of this is bad. It is just the way it is.

Pop Pop has some favorite ways of praying he asked me to share with you.

1. He asks to be shown how to live his life so that he brings peace to everyone, including himself.
2. He asks to see only the good in everyone and to offer love to everyone.
3. He asks to always have all that is needed for a fun life.

He is experiencing many answers to these prayers right now and is having so much fun enjoying these answers.

I would like you to take some time today to pray with Me. All you need do is think of what you really want. Then watch the answers show up. Have fun!

Love,

God

36. Telling the Truth

Dear Jasmine,

There are times when you try to hide things from me.

You even try, at times to hide yourself.

I know this and I know fully what you are trying to hide.

You don't need to do this because there is nothing you can do

or think or say that will ever change my complete love for you.

I love you when you are in the fun of your summer, through the changing colors and falling leaves of autumn, in the quiet coldness and darkness of winter and of course in the beauty of spring.

I am here for you in all the seasons of your life.

Learn to trust. Learn to speak what is the truth.

Always say what you mean and mean what you say, especially when talking to me.

And, you know, when you talk to your friends, your brothers and sister, your mother and father,

Pop Pop , your self, **"Everyone",**

you are speaking to Me.

If you are afraid, pause and ask Me to help you speak the truth.

I will send my angels to help you form the right words.

Love,

37. An Instrument of Peace

Dear Jasmine,

When your Pop Pop was a young man and married to your Nanna Barbara they named one of there children, James Francis Assisi, You know him as Uncle James. They did this because your Pop Pop's favorite prayer was a prayer given to us by a man named Francis who lived in Italy many years ago. He lived in a town called Assisi. His father was a rich merchant and wanted Francis to have all the luxuries the world offered. Francis liked to go out with pretty girls, drink and have fun with his friends. This is very much like your father and your Pop Pop did when they were young.

Francis went off to war with one of his friends. He was what you now think of as an army officer. His friend was very brave and killed many enemy soldiers. Francis was brave but could not stand to kill. He deserted the army and went back to his family in Assisi. His father was very displeased, but Francis told him that he could not kill and was going off to be with the poor people of the town and help them. He gave up all his riches to do this.

He discovered that their churches were all broken up and falling apart. Francis went around begging for money to help the poor rebuild their churches. He wanted them to have a comfortable place to talk to Me. Many young men followed his example and they became know as Franciscan Friars. They still exist today.

Remember a while back I told you about music that Olivia Newton John had recently written. I sent you the words to one of those songs called "Let Go and Let God". Here are the words to another of her songs. This one is based on the prayer that Francis gave us. Pop Pop is sending her new album to you which contains these songs. He would like you to listen and sing these songs with him when he visits you in July.

Instruments of Peace

Where there is hatred, let me bring love
Where there is doubt, let me bring faith,
Where there is falsehood, let me bring truth
Where there is pain, I'll comfort you

Where there is silence, let me sing praise
Where there is despair, let me bring hope
Where there is blindness, let me bring sight
Where there is darkness, let me bring light

And with these words I speak
Grant that I may not seek
To be heard but to hear
To be consoled but to console
Not to be seen, but to see
To be loved, but to love.

For when we give love we will receive.
When we forgive (with) love, we'll find reprieve
It is in dying (to our wants) we'll be released
Make me an instrument of peace.

Love,

God

38. How I Love You

Dear Jasmine,

Do you know how I love you? Do you think I love you only when your room is picked up? Do you think I only love you when you are being obedient to your father and mother? Do you think I only love you when you are kind and loving? Do you think I only love you when you do well in school? If you do, you would be mistaken. I love you just the way you are **at all times**.

This is how I ask you to love.

Love the storms, the hurricanes that come into your life. Love the rainy dark days as much as the bright sunny ones. Love the barking dogs as much as your purring cat.

I am not asking you not to enjoy the things you like.

I am asking you to **enjoy everything**.

I am asking you to trust that everything is perfect just the way it is.

Everything is just unfolding the way I want it to because I know what will bring everyone Home to My Heart. You only see a small portion of My Heart and so you must trust. I see it ALL and I know it is All good. Some day you will see as I see and will no longer need to trust. For now I ask you to trust Me.

With this trust you can breathe freely and walk across the stage of life and present yourself as the perfect being I have created.

Love,

God

39. About Death

Dear Jasmine,

Your father has probably told you that your Nana Barbara only has a few more days to spend on this earth in her body. I want you to know that I am by her side and there are many angels surrounding her. She is fine. Her spirit is strong and she will soon know the joy of letting go of her body and joining with all the spirits who are waiting for her return to the world of pure spirit.

Pop Pop adapted a song that he is sending her to lighten her fear of releasing her body:

Here is what he sent her:

"I adapted the words of a song given to us by Resta somewhat to express my feelings:

Dear Barbara Mary,

The parting of the road is here, different ways to walk to God

If we have chosen different roads it doesn't mean we are lost.

We've taught each other many things that's what our love was for.

Take with you my blessing and I will treasure yours.

I will pray for you every day for you.

I will prayer for you for your highest good.

I will send a smile across all the miles and an angel to give it to you.

Our journey has been sweet sometimes but also stained with tears.

It's easy to lose sight of love though eyes made dark with fears.

You've given me so many gifts of kindness, love and hope.

I want to let you go in peace now that our story's done.

So I will pray for you every day for you.

I will pray for your highest good.

I will send a smile across all the miles and an angel to bring it to you.

Bodies seem to go apart but spirits are ever One.

No matter where we go our love can not be undone.

Christ in you and Christ in me is all we really are.

And while we dream of separate homes we are joined within God's heart.

And I will pray for you every day for you.

I will pray for you for your highest good.

I will send a smile across all the miles and an angel to give to you.

Love,

Michael"

Pop Pop will teach you how to sing this song when he comes up to visit with you in July.

Love, God

40. Your Feelings

Dear Jasmine,

Don't be afraid or ashamed of your feelings.
They are a way to My truth.
It is your feelings that will release you from any darkness you
may experience.
If you have feelings you don't like or want,
like sadness or anger or fear bring them to Me.
Don't try to disguise them.
Don't try to hide them.
My light will shine away any darkness you experience.
Just say something like this to Me:

"Dear Holy Friend, I feel sick. I feel afraid. I feel lonely. I feel
sad. I feel angry. Please help me to stand in the Light of your
Joy and Love.

I will let My presence be known to you.
I will never leave you with feelings that hurt.
But you must bring them to me.
I can't bring you my Light unless you ask for it.
You see, I created you as a being who has free will.
And that includes the will to turn your back on Me.
But remember even with your back turned
I am still and will always remain by your side.

Love,

God

41. I Depend Upon You

Dear Jasmine,

I bet you didn't know how much I depend upon you. I miss you when you are sad. Do you know how much I appreciate your happiness and joy and fun. I cannot experience these feelings without you.

I'm not sad when you are sad but it's kind of like I have to look elsewhere to experience the joy that I command. A part of Me is missing and I feel it. That is why I command joy and happiness. This is My will for us.

It is not selfish to be joyful, happy and to have fun. When you are experiencing these feelings it is never just for you. Joy makes more joy for all of us. Happiness makes more happiness. Fun makes more fun. Find out what it is that makes you joyful, happy and full of fun. Is it drawing, music, writing, being with your friends? Do those things that seem to make you joyful, happy and are fun. Be joyful and happy. Sing your song of joy to the High Heavens. There is no other song Heaven loves as well as this. Make believe you have a garden and joy, happiness and fun are the seeds you are planting. Water these seeds every day with your smiles. Watch them grow.

This is My will for you, because this is My will for myself. Join with Me and make Our wills One will.

Love,

God

42. Guilt

Dear Jasmine,

Did you know that feeling guilty about something is not the same as being guilty? You cannot really be guilty of anything because I made you as innocent and holy and you can't change that.

Often times, however, you feel guilty and try to hide these feelings by being angry, going off alone or refusing to talk or be with other people.

Come to Me at such times and tell me what you are feeling. I promise I will always offer you forgiveness for whatever it is you feel guilty about. Then you will learn to forgive yourself. And if there is someone you need to apologize to, do it. You will quickly feel better if you do these two simple things:

1. Come to Me.
2. Go to your brother or sister with love.

I always know you as innocent no matter what you think of yourself. My forgiveness is just the door you need to go through to experience the true "you" that I know.

Love,

God

43. Giving Away Your Love

Dear Jasmine,

Do you ever get the feeling that things are not quite real, like you are living in a dream. If this happens to you don't be frightened. It only means you are getting closer to Me. You see, when I see you, you are asleep. I come to you in your day time and nighttime dreams. I come to you when the world doesn't seem quite real to you.

That's why I tell you not to hold too tightly to the things you treasure in your world. They are only parts of your dream. When you wake up fully they will disappear.

The only thing to hold onto is the love you feel for your mother, father, brothers, sister, friends, Pop Pop, Nanny Connie and everything else you love. Only hold the love in your heart briefly and then give it away, because even the love can't be known unless you give it away. Life is meant to be alive, to constantly change in marvelous ways, ways that you can't imagine until you are willing to give away whatever you think you love.

Today see how much love you can give away. I'll be there playing right along with you.

Love you so so much,

God

44. Getting What You Truly Want

Dear Jasmine,

You understand what it means to be willful, do you not? When people say you are willful they mean that you want things your own way and will do anything to get what you want. Generally this is not a complement. But did you know that I am willful, too.

I want things to be a certain way for you and I am not happy when they are not the way I want. I have everything I want so My will applies only to you. Here is My will for you: that you be genuinely happy through and through, content, feeling like you have everything you want, at peace all the time, feel you can have and be whatever you desire, and know that you are responsible for your life.

Wouldn't you like Me to always get My way? I'll tell you a secret, if you are willing to join your will with Mine we will both be getting what we want all the time. Wouldn't that be fun? And you know what? Nobody else would have to give anything to us. Things would just come to us like we were a happiness magnet.

So you see, I like it when you are willful. Most adults have lost the power of their will and give in to what other people want too much. I want you to desire strongly to see that what you want comes true for you. Of course, I don't want you to get what you want by forcing someone to give it to you. I don't want you to steal it from someone. What I want is for you to join your will with My will. We make an unbeatable team.

Love Ya',

God

45. You Are a Star

Dear Jasmine,

Do you know why I blessed you with birth? I wanted you to be my star. I wanted you to star in the play you call your life. Every word, every action in this play has been scripted by Me. It is written so that you can shine My Love onto the earth and back to the heavens. All you need do is to be willing to let my Light shine. Don't block it by the density of fear. Trust in what I tell you now and know that all fear will disappear in the Love that radiates from your being. Trust in what I allow you to see, feel and experience and know that it is all good when you view it with love.

When you are afraid or unsure of your star quality come to Me. I am always here for you but I allow you to hide from the brightness of your star light for as long as you wish. I know that one day you will come out from hiding. I want you to know that when you do, it's party time. Why wait? Come join us for the fun now.

Love you now and always,

God

46. Your One Creation

Dear Jasmine,

Did you know that I have only One creation? Want to know what it is? I bet you do.

You are My only creation. This is true even though it doesn't seem this way. That's because I created you to be just like Me, capable of doing anything at all, capable of making anything at all, capable of being perfectly happy all the time, capable of being sad or mad if that is what you desire to experience. All the stuff you see is part of your creation. All the stuff you experience is part of your creation.

You will realize that you are My One perfect creation as you realize that whatever you experience is what you asked to experience. Learn to love your experiences. Don't label them as good or bad, right or wrong. Just love them. Be with those that are difficult just like I suggested you be with difficult people. The more you do this the happier you will be. The more you do this the more you will realize how much I love you and how much you love them. The more you do this the more you will realize that you have only One creation as well. All you experience will become this One creation.

I cannot live without you. You are that important to Me. You cannot live without your creation. It is that important to you. When you love all things you experience you come to know that what I am saying to you is true. Start today to love all that happens to you. And most of all don't label anything, just experience it as fully as you can. I will be there to help you when you forget or when things seem hard to take. Just call Me when this seems hard for you to do.

My love never leaves you and some day your love will never leave your creation.

Your forever friend,

God

47. The Two Horses

Dear Jasmine,

Here is a true story one of my angels wrote. I know you will enjoy it and get the message it contains. I also included a poem Pop Pop wrote to go with this story.

"Just up the road from my house is a field, with two horses in it.
From distance, each looks like every other horse. But if you stop
your car, or you are walking by, you will notice something quite amazing.

Looking into the eyes of one horse will disclose that he is blind.
His owner has chosen not to have him put down, but make a good home
for him. This alone is amazing.

If nearby and listening, you will hear the sound of a bell. Looking
around for the source of the sound, you will see that is comes from
the smaller horse in the field. Attached to her halter is a small

bell. It lets her blind friend know where she is, so he can follow her.

As you stand and watch these two friends, you'll see how she is always

checking on him, and that he will listen for her bell and then slowly

walk to where she is, trusting that she will not lead him astay. When

she returns to the shelter of the barn each evening, she stops

occasionally and looks back, making sure her friend isn't too far

behind to hear the bell.

Like the owners of these two horses, God does not throw us away

because we are not perfect or because we have problems of challenges.

He watches over us and even brings others into our lives to help us

when we are in need.

Sometimes we are the blind horse being guided by the little ringing

bell of those who God places in our lives.

Other times we are the guide horse, helping others see.

Good friends are like this. You don't always see them, but you know

they are always there.

Please listen for my bell and I'll listen for yours."

Be kinder and more loving than necessary, for everyone you meet is trying very hard to find their way home to Me.

Your friend,

God

heart to heart

I see the light
and point it out
looking about expecting
you to see it too
i am disappointed
in your blank response
but its so bright
can't you see its shining
and lighting home
for you and me
but then i notice a haze
about your eyes
you cannot see
what is so plain to me
i step a back and touch my heart
and place my hand on yours.
it beats as mine
and longs to see
what i am so enthralled about
a voice says dear
you see so far
but miss on what is near
this other loves you so
but has not yet allowed himself
to feel the grandness that you preach
just put this bell about your neck
and ring it patiently

as you walk to home
take little steps looking back
to see your friend
don't go to far from him
unless he turns and walks away
 take small steps
to guide his path
enjoying love
that's here to stay

Michael

48. Happy Birthday

Dear Jasmine,

Your birthday party was great. Thanks for having Me there. Your smiles and joy was so obvious to all. Pop Pop told me the gift you gave him of the shell with the smiley face on it. You told him you wanted him to have it because he smiles all the time. Now you are doing that, too. Love and joy is so contagious. You both have Me smiling as well.

I know you really liked the wallet that Nonny Connie gave you. And I bet you liked the money Pop Pop put in it. If you ever think you need more just ask Me. I love for you to have all the money you ever want or think you need. Just ask and I'll send it to you.

And, you got a new saxophone from your Dad. He loves you so, and you know it even when he is a bit blustery. Do what Pop Pop does when he is like that, just smile at him and know that that is his way of showing love. There are tons of ways for people to show their love.

Pop Pop told you about the meaning of your new age, eleven. It is a sign of divinity and new beginnings. Use the hand on your head exercise he showed you to bring this divinity into your mind. The spinning exercise that he showed you and Paul, Jr can also help you be smarter than you already are.

I was so pleased to see you be so loving to your brother, Paul. You certainly are setting a good example for your brothers and sister.

I guess you can tell I am so proud of you.

Your Pal,

God

Reflections on a Recent Visit from My Son and His Family

Love has no form
But, Tracey's smile and her kiss
stirs my soul.
Her loving care for her children
delights me.
Jasmine's and young Paul's willingness to learn
Excites me.
Connie's playing ball with young Paul
pleases me.
My son, Paul's, cooking and caring for all
invites me
And Jade and Jacob's holding Teacup,
our small dog
And shouting cheers that Pop Pop
and Nonnie Connie rock
Knocks off my socks.
Yet love has no form.

Michael

Jasmine's Letter to Pop Pop

December 30,2007

Dear Pop Pop,

You'll never guess what happened just because I listened to my favorite radio station, 92.7:WOBM, this morning. I heard Bob Levy's Topic A about a families house being burnt down. There's a mother, a father, a 6-year old boy, a 4-year old girl, and a 2- year old girl and a cat. There was a dog but the dog died in the fire. Other than the cat they lost everything: including all the gifts that Christmas. So there was this donation for the family and I just had to help out. So I called the radio station and made it onto the radio to get the address for the donation.

It turned out that it was at the radio station. It was easy to donate for us because we had unwanted gifts of duplicates and there were all those stuffed animals of mine up in the attic. We also donatd two bags of clothing. And last but not least we donated the book you gave me. I wrote on the inside cover"My Pop Pop wrote this book. When I'm sad my Pop Pop always cheers me up. I hope he can do the same for you." We(my Dad and I) wrote two cards and attached them to your book.

Mine was on the front and said, "Although the fire was so hot, it brought to you this gift. All the pain this Chrismas brought I hope that pain soon lifts."

Dad's was on the back of your book and said. Well, I forgot what he wrote.

(She drew a picture here)

Please write back soon!

JAZ + (Yin, my cat)

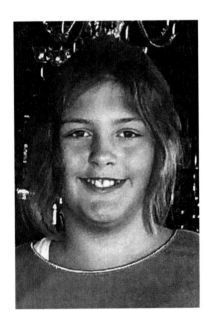

Made in the USA